I Spy
with My Little
Eye
Baseball

Photographs by **David Milne** and text by **Brad Herzog**

Fun for all ages!

Sleeping Bear Press

To my wonderful family for all their love and support.

D. M.

To my niece Beatrice and my nephew Eli. I spy two adorable redheads.

B. H.

David Milne would like to thank:
Bruce Rodgers
Adam Bissonnette
Ray, Matt and Chris Parker
Gregory Bria, Oakwood Sports
Art Katsapis
Ron Townshend
Dave and Erin Guliani
Ward & Patch Sports
Louisville Slugger
R. Lanctot Group, Quebec
Mike Bernard
Michigan State University
Jim Petselis
Lindsay Milne
Christian Davila
Ron Belluomini, Coach Oakville Bantam AAA
Samantha Currie
Jim Findlay (3rd base coach)
Nick Rico
The Trophy Centre, Toronto
Irene Crichton
Nick Shanks
Iain Faulkner

Text Copyright © 2011 Brad Herzog
Photographs Copyright © 2011 David Milne

Sleeping Bear Press™

315 East Eisenhower Parkway, Suite 200
Ann Arbor, MI 48108
www.sleepingbearpress.com

Sleeping Bear Press is an imprint of Gale, a part of Cengage Learning.

10 9 8 7 6 5 4 3 2 1

Library of Congress Cataloging-in-Publication Data
Herzog, Brad.
I spy with my little eye Baseball / written by Brad Herzog; photos by David Milne.
p. cm.
ISBN 978-1-58536-496-1
1. Baseball—Juvenile literature. 2. Picture puzzles—Juvenile literature. I. Milne, David, photographer . II. Title. III. Title: Baseball.
GV867.5.H466 2011
796.357—dc22
2010013370

Printed by China Translation & Printing Services Limited, Guangdong Province, China. 1st printing. 11/2010

I spy with my little eye two pictures that look just the same.
An identical view isn't always what's true.
Find the changes to play this game.

 Now let's get started...

I spy with my little eye baseball bats—metal and wood.
Keep your eye on each ball. Can you count them all?
Would a shoe walk away if it could?

Find at Least
15
Changes

Photo Fact: The most famous baseball bat model in the world is the Louisville Slugger. According to legend, the very first one was created in 1884 for major league player Pete Browning after he broke one of his bats. The Louisville Slugger company's original bat model was known as the Falls City Slugger (because Louisville, Kentucky, is located at the Falls of the Ohio River). By the 1920s more than one million Louisville Sluggers were being produced each year. Today, in front of the Louisville Slugger Museum, there stands a 120-foot-tall baseball bat, the largest in the world. Inside the building is a 15-ton sculpture of a mitt and a ball.

I spy with my little eye a coach giving signs to his team.
Touch your ear, tap your chest. His players know best
that those signals mean more than they seem.

Find at Least **16** Changes

 **Photo Fact:** In the quiet time between pitches during a baseball game, there may be quite a bit of sign language happening. A catcher may give a sign to a pitcher about what to throw. A fastball? A curveball? A pitchout? A manager may give a sign to a third-base coach, who will convey the message to the batter. Should he bunt? Take a pitch without swinging? Swing away? The base coach may also give a sign to a runner about whether he should steal or not. These signs often consist of a series of movements that are confusing to most observers, but they make sense to the players receiving the signs because they know what to look for.

I spy with my little eye eleven fine gloves and mitts.
Some are old, some brand new, some barely will do.
Try one on. See which one of them fits.

Find at Least
20
Changes

Photo Fact: Although the words "glove" and "mitt" are often used to describe the same piece of equipment, mitts (like those used by catchers and first basemen) do not have individual fingers. They are more like mittens. There are hundreds of models of baseball gloves to choose from these days, but in the earliest days of baseball most players didn't wear any gloves at all. The last major-leaguer to field without a glove was Jerry Denny, a third baseman who retired in 1894. At that time, most gloves simply consisted of leather padding to protect the palms of the fielders' hands. Their fingers weren't even covered!

I spy with my little eye equipment tossed in a pile.
There's more gum to chew, and an altered shoe.
A batting glove gets a new style.

Find at Least
24
Changes

I spy with my little eye a bevy of baseballs with stitches.
If you want to win, just watch the balls spin.
Can you hit what the pitcher pitches?

Photo Fact: The baseball has experienced very few changes since the game's early days. Since 1872 the official Major League Baseball has weighed about five ounces and has measured nine inches around. It consists of a cork center wrapped tightly in wool and yarn and covered by cowhide. The two parts of the cover are hand sewn together (with exactly 108 stitches) using precisely 88 inches of red thread. The final people to prepare the baseballs are the umpires. Brand new balls are too slick and shiny to use, so before each game the umpires rub each ball with a substance—Lena Blackburne Baseball Rubbing Mud—from a special (and secret) mud hole in New Jersey.

I spy with my little eye a bunch of really close plays.
A scoreboard that's strange, numbers that change,
and a slide taken two different ways.

HOMER STRYKER FIELD

#10 A. McWilliams
AVG. .281 HR 3 RBI 16

AT BAT		BALL		STRIKE		OUT		H/E

DAKTRONICS

	1	2	3	4	5	6	7	8	9	10	RUNS	HITS	ERR
VISITOR	1	1	0								3		0
HOME	3	0									3		3

BASEBALL.
HOT DOGS.
ROCK & ROLL.

FM103 WKFR PLAYS THE HITS!

FM103 WKFR PLAYS THE HITS!

Find at Least **41** *Changes*

Photo Fact: In 1845 an amateur baseball club in New York City created the Knickerbocker Rules of baseball. Among other things, the new rules limited the number of bases to four, set them in the shape of a diamond and fixed them at 90 feet apart (little league bases are 60 feet apart). Even as hitters and fielders continue to improve, 90 feet appears to be the perfect distance for professional baseball games. The distance is why a ground ball to the third baseman always seems to result in a close play and why it is usually a matter of inches when a runner tries to steal second base. The Knickerbockers knew what they were doing!

I spy with my little eye concentration on a batter's face.
Check the scoreboard once more. Wait, what's the score?
Is he safe or out at second base?

Find at Least **18** Changes

Photo Fact: Modern scoreboards come equipped with all sorts of gadgets. But the first man to see a scoreboard's entertainment potential was a fun-loving fellow named Bill Veeck. As the owner of the Chicago White Sox in 1960, he installed the first "exploding scoreboard," which produced fireworks when the home team hit home runs. Veeck was famous for creating many hilarious promotional stunts. Once, when he owned a team in St. Louis, he let the fans act as managers for a day. During the game a man held up cards with proposed moves (such as "bunt" or "change pitchers"). The spectators replied with cards that said "yes" or "no." Meanwhile, the real manager relaxed in a rocking chair. The St. Louis Browns won the game!

I spy with my little eye a colorful cardboard collection.
Pennants switch places, the cards get new faces,
and a Tiger changes direction.

Photo Fact: Baseball cards have been collected by boys and girls for many decades, mostly for fun. But some cards can be quite valuable. The most valuable baseball card—known as the T206 Honus Wagner card—is more than 100 years old. Wagner was a shortstop, an eight-time batting champion, and one of the first five players elected to the National Baseball Hall of Fame. There are fewer than sixty T206 cards in existence, and one of them was once owned by legendary hockey star Wayne Gretzky. In 2007 that particular card sold for nearly $3 million!

I spy with my little eye baseball books and stars' autographs.
Look closely at a few. Is that one batter or two?
The changes may cause a few laughs.

Find at Least **36** Changes

Photo Fact: The first book devoted entirely to baseball is believed to be the *Base Ball Player's Pocket Companion*, which was published in 1859 (in those days "baseball" was usually divided into two words). It is estimated that fewer than a dozen copies of this book still exist. Since then, baseball has become the most popular sport among book collectors. Thousands of baseball books have been published over the years, including *The Baseball Encyclopedia*, which provides statistics for every man who has ever played Major League Baseball. The book is more than 3,000 pages long and weighs more than eight pounds!

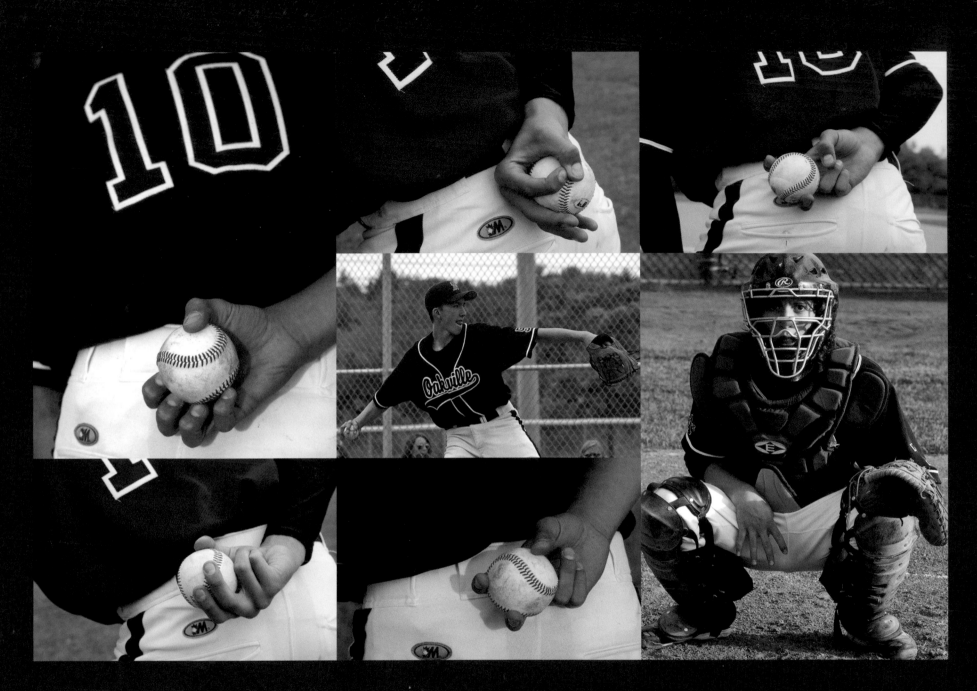

I spy with my little eye a pitcher preparing to throw.
Hold the ball just right, but that's a strange sight!
How many fingers does he show?

Photo Fact: The type of pitch thrown depends on how a pitcher grips a ball, where the fingers are placed, how the ball is released, and how hard it is thrown. Most young kids usually throw a fastball or perhaps a changeup (which is thrown with the same motion as a fastball, but at a lower speed). However, many older players learn to throw other kinds of pitches, including the curveball, knuckleball, forkball, slider, sinker, and split-fingered fastball. The Eephus pitch, a rarely used trick pitch, moves barely half as fast as the speediest fastballs. It is sometimes known as the Bugs Bunny curve, which refers to cartoons in which a batter swings three times before the pitch arrives at home plate.

I spy with my little eye an umpire making a call.
He's the man in blue, but the colors change, too,
when he says "stee-rike!" or "ball."

Find at Least
24
Changes

Photo Fact: Although most little league games use two umpires, four umpires work major league games (six in the all-star game and play-offs). However, in the earliest days of baseball (back in the 1850s), each game had only one umpire. If the ump was unable to see a play, he sometimes asked the spectators for advice on a call! The umpire is often called the "man in blue," but in 1972 a woman named Bernice Gera became the first female umpire in professional baseball. Another important first happened in 1956—the year that two men became the first major league umpires to wear glasses on the field!

I spy with my little eye trophies of all shapes and sizes.
Did those ribbons and medals come with engines and pedals?
There's movement among all those prizes.

Photo Fact: Every year, the winner of the World Series receives the Commissioner's Trophy, which was first awarded to the St. Louis Cardinals in 1967. A new trophy is created each year. The current version features 30 gold-plated flags, one for each team in Major League Baseball. The World Series pits the American League champion against the National League champ. Today, it is a best-of-seven series, meaning the first team to win four games (out of a maximum of seven) is the winner. The very first series in 1903 and three others (in 1919, 1920, and 1921) were best-of-nine series.

I spy with my little eye bobbleheads on a pitcher's mound.
Their uniforms change hue, and there's one mascot who
seems to be moving around.

Find at Least **30** Changes

Photo Fact: Almost every Major League Baseball team has a mascot—a costumed figure who roams the ballpark and performs silly routines for the crowd. The first modern-day mascot is believed to have been Mr. Met, who looks like a man with a large baseball-shaped head. He was introduced to New York Mets fans in 1964. Two of the most famous baseball mascots, the San Diego Chicken and the Phillie Phanatic, are credited with popularizing the use of mascots in the major leagues. Now there are mascots of all kinds—including the Pirate Parrot, Billy the Marlin, and Mariner Moose.

I spy with my little eye a team's jerseys hung in a row.
A bat upside down, a helmet turned 'round.
And those name tags—where did they go?

Photo Fact: For the first several decades of organized baseball, teams didn't put uniform numbers on their players' jerseys. It was difficult to tell who was who! Numbered jerseys started to become popular when the great New York Yankees teams of the 1920s and 1930s used them. At that time, a player's number was usually related to his place in the batting lineup. For instance, New York slugger Babe Ruth (who batted third) wore #3, and Lou Gehrig (who batted fourth) wore #4. Gehrig was the first player in Major League Baseball to have his uniform number retired by his team, meaning no other Yankee has ever worn it.

David Milne is a third-generation photographer in Toronto, Canada. His grandfather, Charles, started Milne Studios in Toronto in 1925. When David completed his schooling at Brooks Institute of Photography in Santa Barbara, California, he returned home to the family business. Currently David is an active photographer for numerous art galleries and artists, corporate portraits, products, and all types of events. David was also the photographer for *I Spy with My Little Eye: Hockey* published by Sleeping Bear Press.

This is *Brad Herzog's* third baseball-themed book after the wildly successful *H is for Home Run: A Baseball Alphabet* and *Full Count: A Baseball Number Book*. He is also the author of several other books for Sleeping Bear Press, including *S is for Save the Planet: A How-to-be Green Alphabet* and *T is for Touchdown: A Football Alphabet*. Brad has published more than two dozen books, including three memoirs on his travels through small-town America.

Brad Herzog lives on California's Monterey Peninsula with his wife Amy and his two sons, Luke and Jesse. As a freelance writer, Brad has won several awards from the Council for Advancement and Support of Education, including a Grand Gold Medal for best magazine article of the year. More information about Brad's books and his school visit program can be found at www.bradherzog.com.